T0144968

Balboa Press books may be ordered through booksellers or by contacting:

Balboa Press
A Division of Hay House
1663 Liberty Drive
Bloomington, IN 47403
www.balboapress.com
844-682-1282

ISBN: 979-8-7652-2826-5 (sc)
ISBN: 979-8-7652-2872-2 (hc)
ISBN: 979-8-7652-2827-2 (e)

Print information available on the last page.

Balboa Press rev. date: 05/04/2022

BALBOA.PRESS
A DIVISION OF HAY HOUSE

When I look around and
I don't see a flower to be found,

I turn inward and make a flower in my mind.

I keep this thought and look for the peace amongst the war.

People emotionally yelling.

People sadly crying.

People nervously waiting.

Find the peace in war.

Create the peace
within your mind.

Look for the helpers. In every hard situation you will see the love and compassion of those people who help.

From the first responders to the volunteering citizens. Watch as they go the extra mile to lend a helping hand to all in need.

It is a natural human instinct to help our neighbors, just as a mother tends to her young, or a child cares for their aging parents. The circle of life is the circle of love.

From the elderly people
to the youngsters playing
around. You can reach inside
to find the peace in war.

Observe the chaos around and put the peace back in the world; it can be found. Be that helpful person, be that smile for your friend, mother, father or brother.

People angrily fighting.
Find the middle.

People emotionally yelling.
Find the love.

People sadly crying.
Find the new life.

17

Find the peace in war.

We create wars in our hearts.
We create fights over who is right.
We create our thoughts and they become our reality.

If our thoughts become real, find the peace in war and let that become our world.

We can see war for what it truly is. War is anger. Observe the sadness but don't allow it to stay all day. Change the sadness into an action that creates peace.

Look to see the helpers within the war
bringing peace with small and big actions.

See the helpers and you will see the peace. Be a helper and you will be an important piece of the community puzzle.

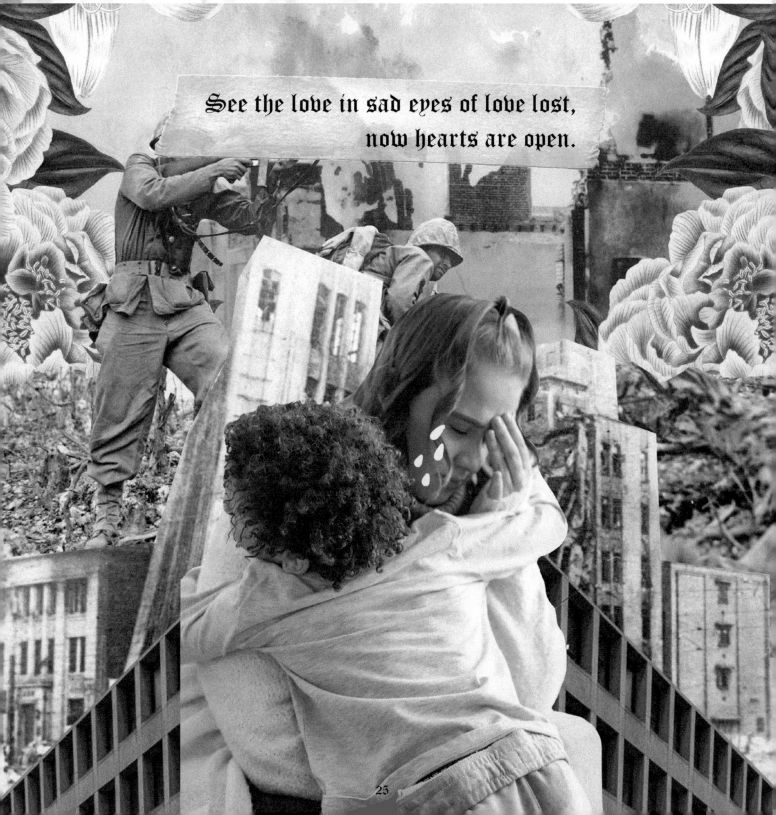

See the love in sad eyes of love lost,
now hearts are open.

See the anger as the emotions,
caring so deeply about one another.

Stay!

See the ones yelling out their feelings - they are passionate.

See the ones nervous in the unknown and embrace the new adventures ahead.

In the midst of war see past the tragedy, the hurt, the loss, and the sadness. Then bring peace, bring joy, bring love, bring compassion.

You are the most powerful one because your thoughts and your actions will bring peace, bring joy, bring love, and bring compassion.

The most powerful super power is peace and love. Wars do not exist when there is peace in your heart.

You create
your reality.
Let's create a
peaceful world
with love, not
war.

Printed in the United States
by Baker & Taylor Publisher Services